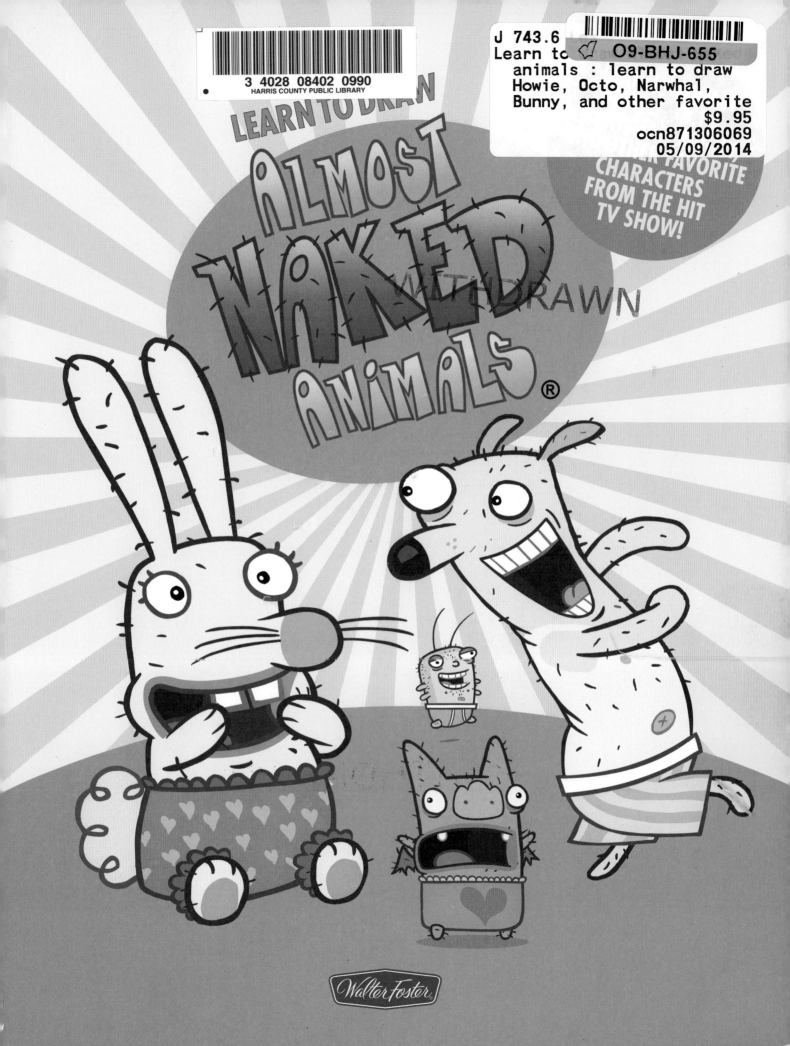

LEARN TO DRAW

ALMOST NAKED ANIMALS®

CHARACTERS
FROM THE HIT
TV SHOW!

Walter Foster

Step-by-step illustrations by Kristina Burr.

1 3 5 7 9 10 8 6 4 2

TABLE OF CONTENTS

MEET THE ALMOST NAKED ANIMALS

WELCOME TO THE BANANA CABANA!

Inside this beachfront tropical hotel, every day is an adventure crazier than the last! The fun-loving staff of animals who work here are full of personality and energy—which they need to keep up with the shenanigans that take place around here. You'll meet everyone inside the pages of this book, but here's a brief rundown of what you can expect as a guest at the Banana Cabana...

Leading the pack is Howie, the hospitality-challenged canine manager. Though he can some-times be a little preoccupied, with the help of his friends, Howie successfully accomplishes—for the most part—the busy job of taking care of his employees and guests.

BANANA CABANA

Upon arrival, you'll be greeted by Octo, the front desk clerk. Don't be alarmed if he seems a little freaked out. Octo is usually an eight-tentacled stress-case—try to keep him from hyperventilating if he accidentally forgets one tiny detail about your reservation.

LOBBY

After you check in, Sloth will make sure your bags get to your room safe and sound—but it may take a while. Sloth moves sweetly along at her own pace. Plan accordingly.

If you need to schedule any activities during your stay, you'll want to meet with Bunny. Hyperactive and short-tempered, she gets the job done. Just agree with everything she says and don't make her mad... ever.

All delicious meals at the Banana Cabana come from the kitchen of Chef Piggy. He is both passionate and ninja-trained—a combination resulting in the occasional angry outburst and more than one type of chopping.

For entertainment, visit the hotel lounge. Narwhal is the star of the current show and, well, every show. As the resident performer, he loves to show guests a good time. Some say he's a bit self-absorbed, but he sure can sing!

If anything in your room needs to be fixed, call Duck. He may be blissfully oblivious to a lot, but this handy-bird is your go-to guy for the problem you never knew you had and the random solution that somehow works perfectly.

Turn the page to join in on the fun!

ENJOY YOUR STAY!

TOOLS & MATERIALS

Before you begin drawing, you will need to gather the right tools. Start with a regular pencil, an eraser, and a pencil sharpener. When you're finished sketching, you can bring your favorite Almost Naked Animal to life by adding color with felt-tip markers, colored pencils, crayons, or even paint!

eraser

sharpener

drawing pencil
and paper

colored pencils

felt-tip
markers

paintbrush
and paints

GETTING STARTED

Professional artists draw characters in steps. The key is to start with simple shapes and gradually add the details. The blue lines will help guide you through the process.

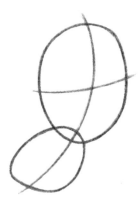

STEP 1

First draw the basic shapes using light lines that will be easy to erase.

STEP 2

Each new step is shown in blue, so you'll know what to add next.

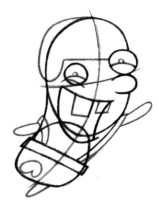

STEP 3

Follow the blue lines to draw the details.

STEP 4

Now darken the lines you want to keep, and erase the rest.

STEP 5

Use (crayons or markers) to add color to your drawing!

SIZE CHART

Howie   Octo   Bunny   Duck   Piggy

Narwhal   Sloth   **Poodle**   **Batty**

HOWIE

As manager of the Banana Cabana, Howie never shies away from a challenge or a chance to be in the spotlight, whether or not he is prepared for it! Always super confident and enthusiastic, Howie is a fan of trampolines and running fast—and dreams of one day becoming a world-famous stunt dog.

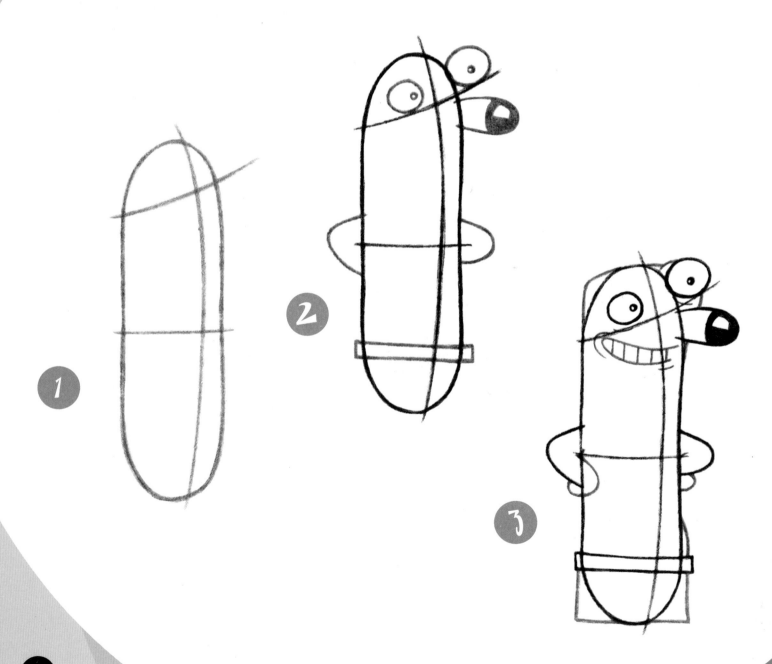

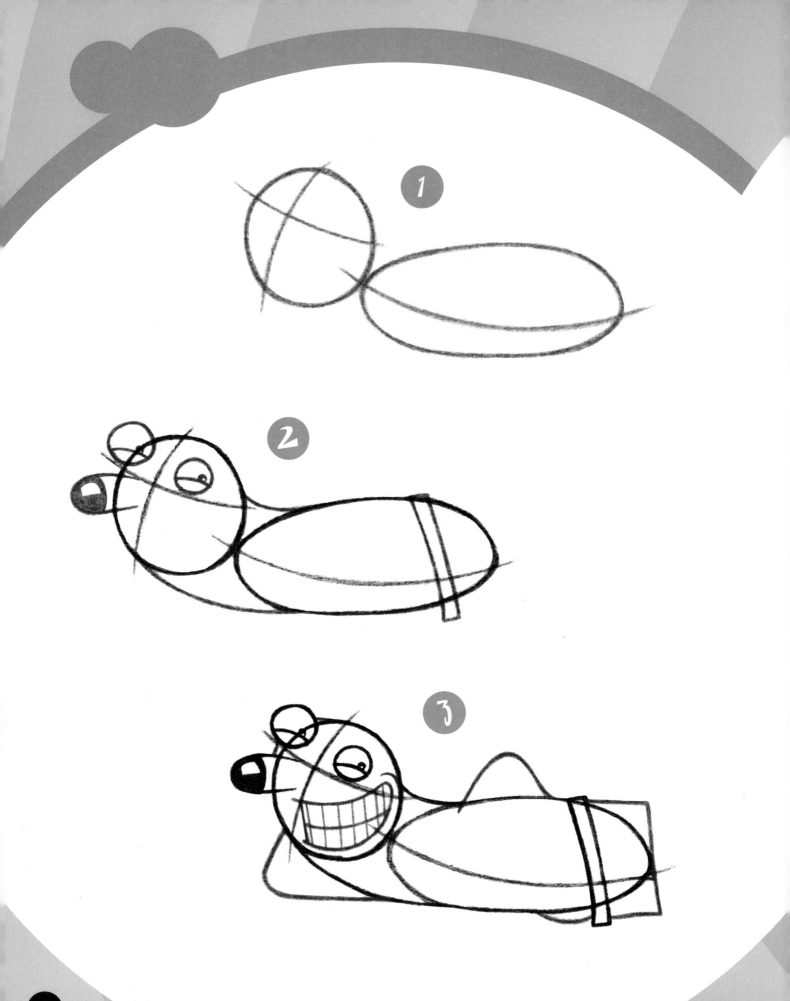

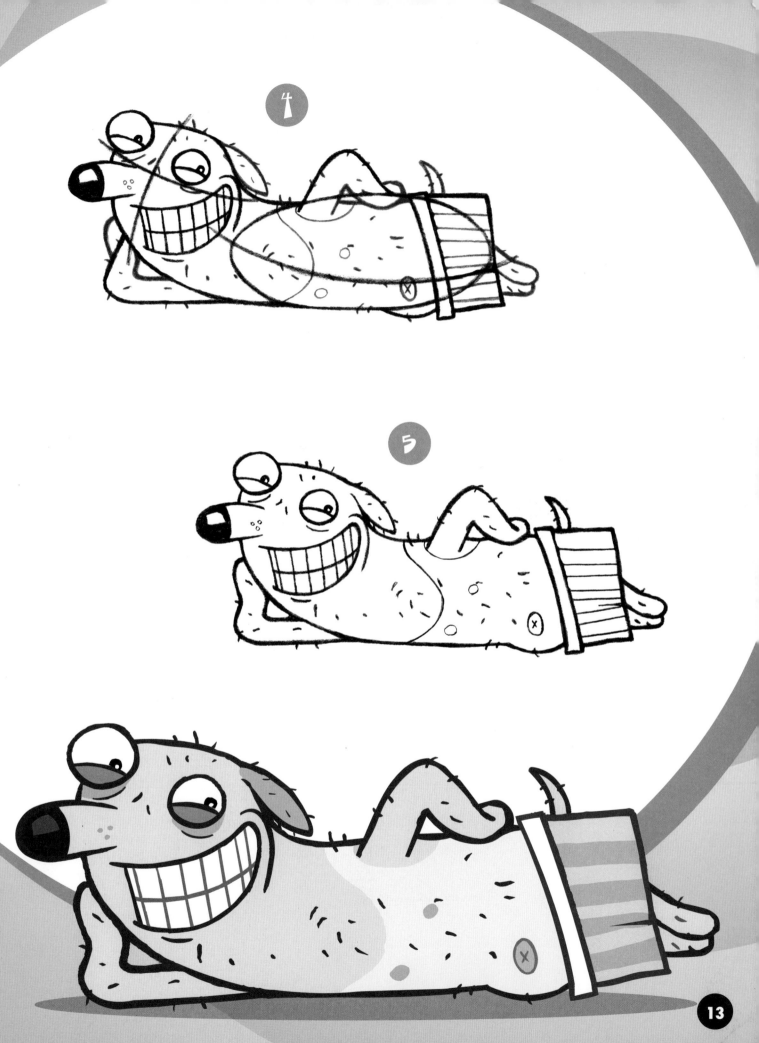

TRY MORE OF HOWIE'S LOOKS!

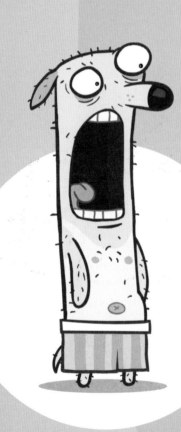

"WHAT COULD POSSIBLY GO WRONG?!"

OCTO

Octo is usually jittery and nervous, and it shows. As the hotel's front desk clerk, Octo tries his best to be the voice of reason, but being afraid of anything and everything tends to land him in a state of flailing, blubbery panic.

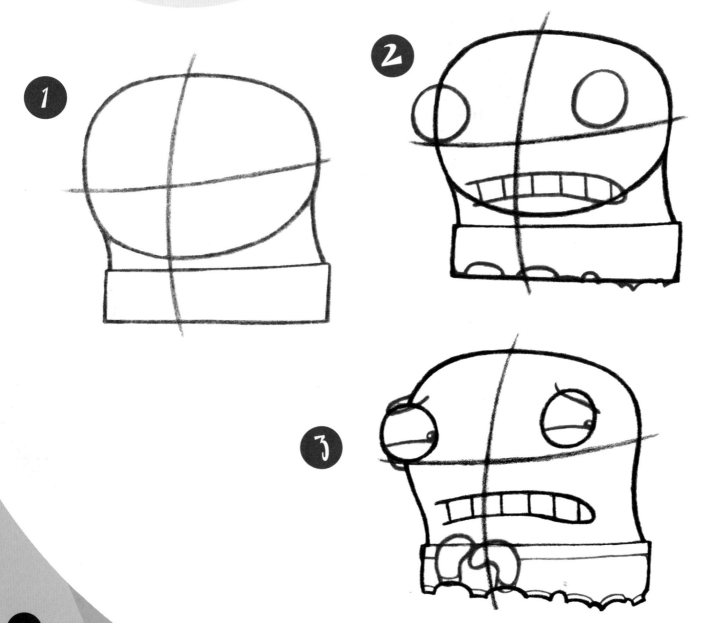

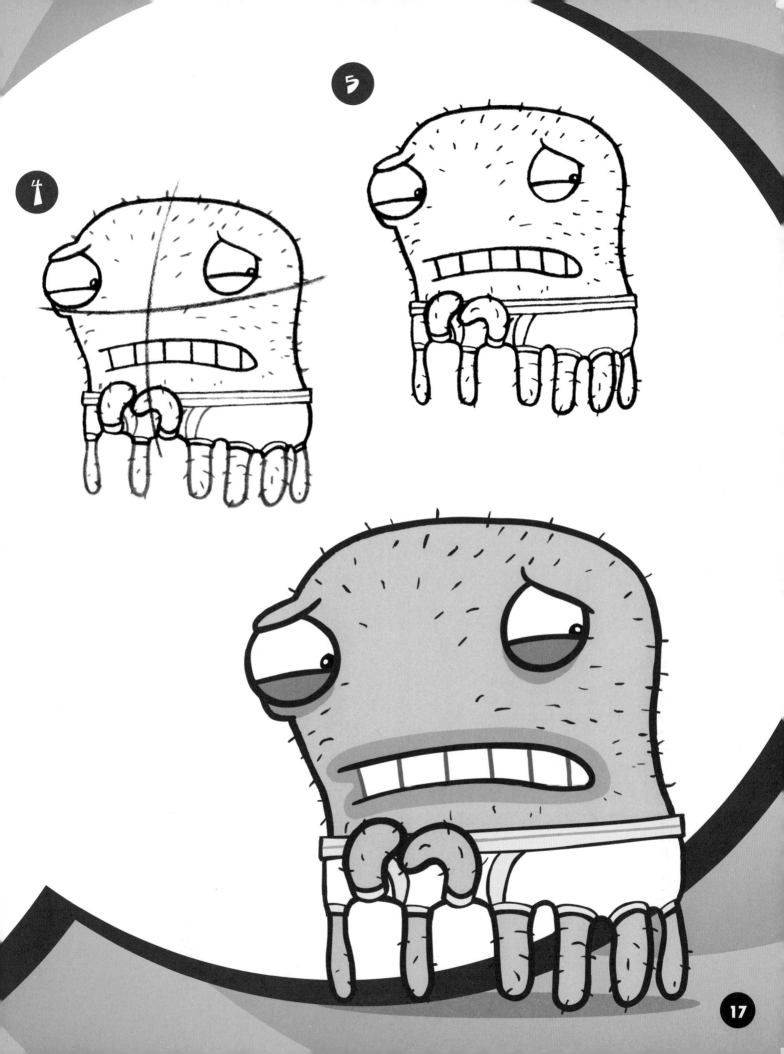

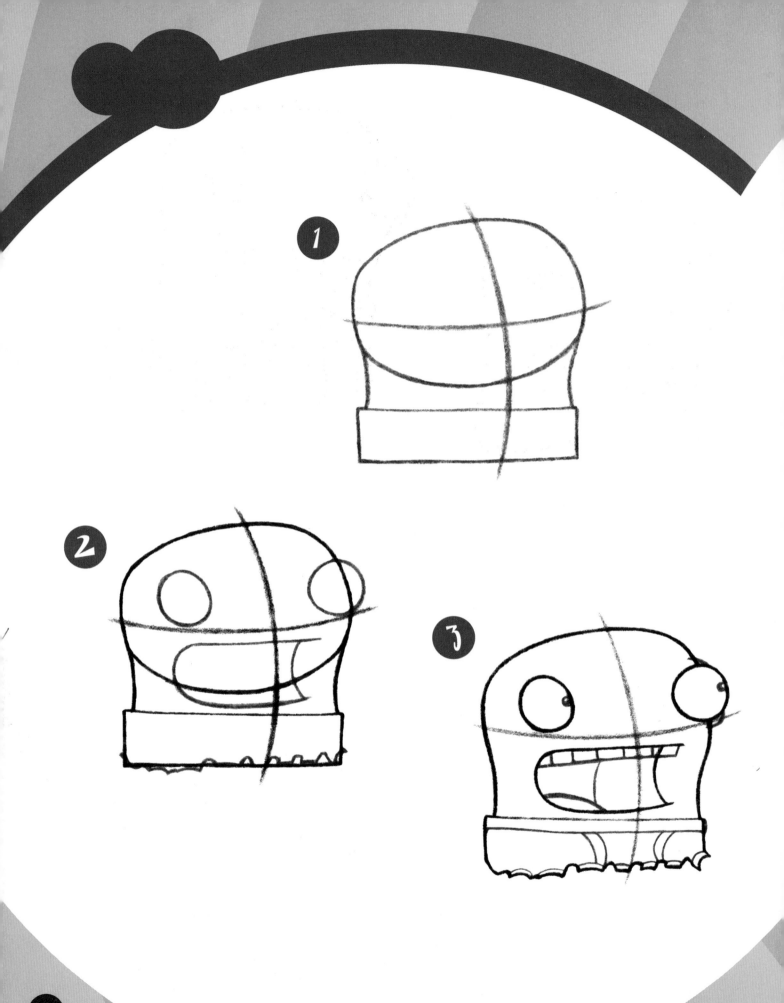

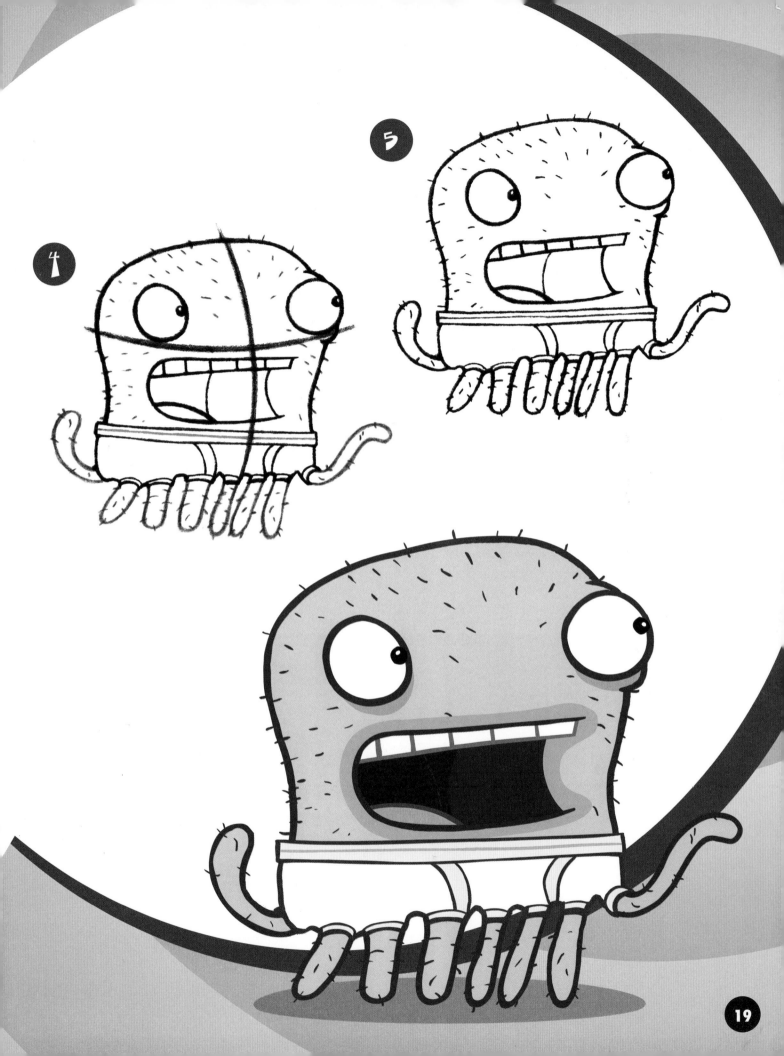

19

TRY MORE OF OCTO'S LOOKS!

"I'LL GO GET MY FIRST AID KIT."

21

DUCK

Known by his friends for being random, overeager, and willing to try anything, Duck is talented in the most unexpected of ways—such as building an artificial sun when the weather goes bad, for example. Accomplishments like this have made him the "duck-of-all-trades" at the hotel, working a variety of odd jobs.

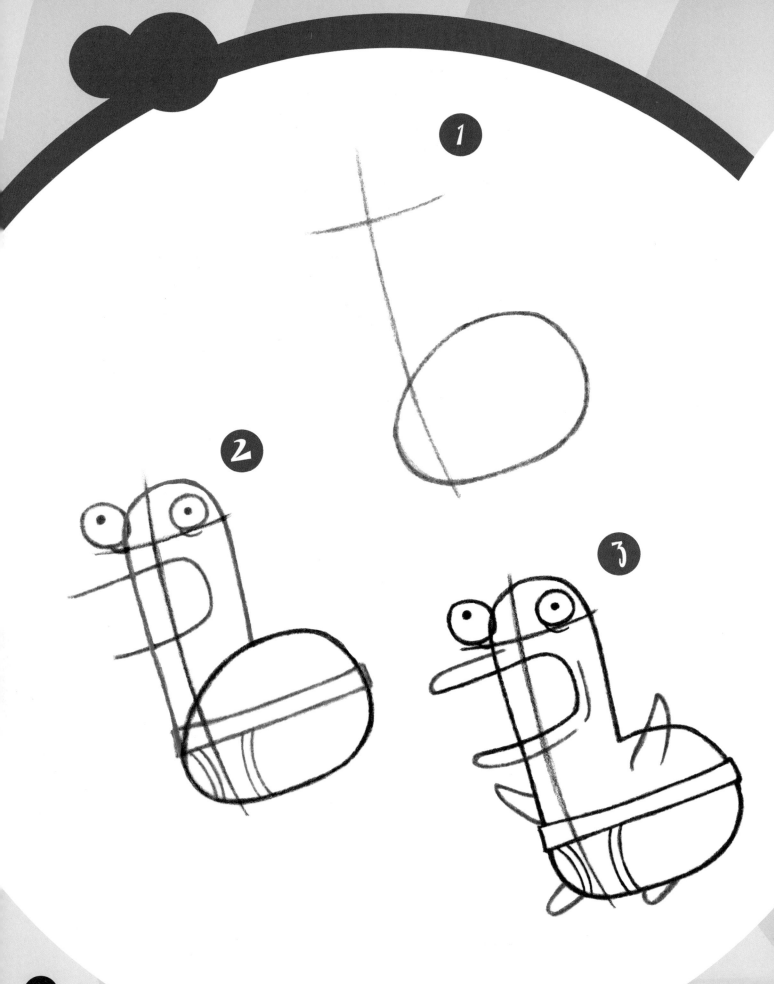

TRY MORE OF DUCK'S LOOKS!

"NICEY!"

BUNNY

Bunny is the hotel's activities director and resident perfectionist. She can be sugary-sweet—with the energy of a cheerleader who has chugged a whole case of Cap'n Fizzy's Fuzzy Orange Soda—but will show major attitude if things don't go her way. Bunny loves attention and lots of activity, as well as princesses, stickers, and rainbows.

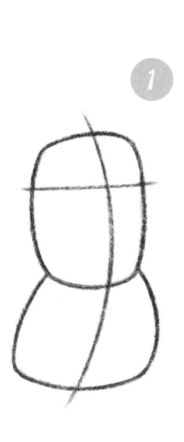

TRY MORE OF BUNNY'S LOOKS!

"THIS CAN'T POSSIBLY END WELL."

NARWHAL

Narwhal can usually be found on stage entertaining Banana Cabana guests by bellowing out showtunes. Equal parts cheese and charm, Narwhal is a true performer, full of drama and passionate emotion—especially when it comes to gazing at the love of his life... in the mirror.

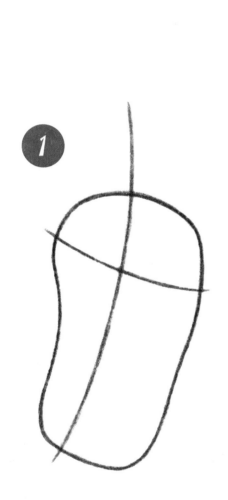

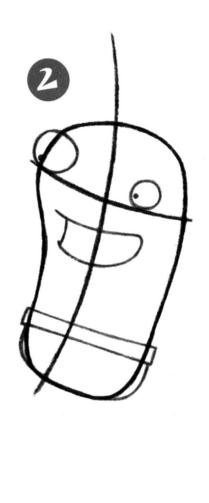

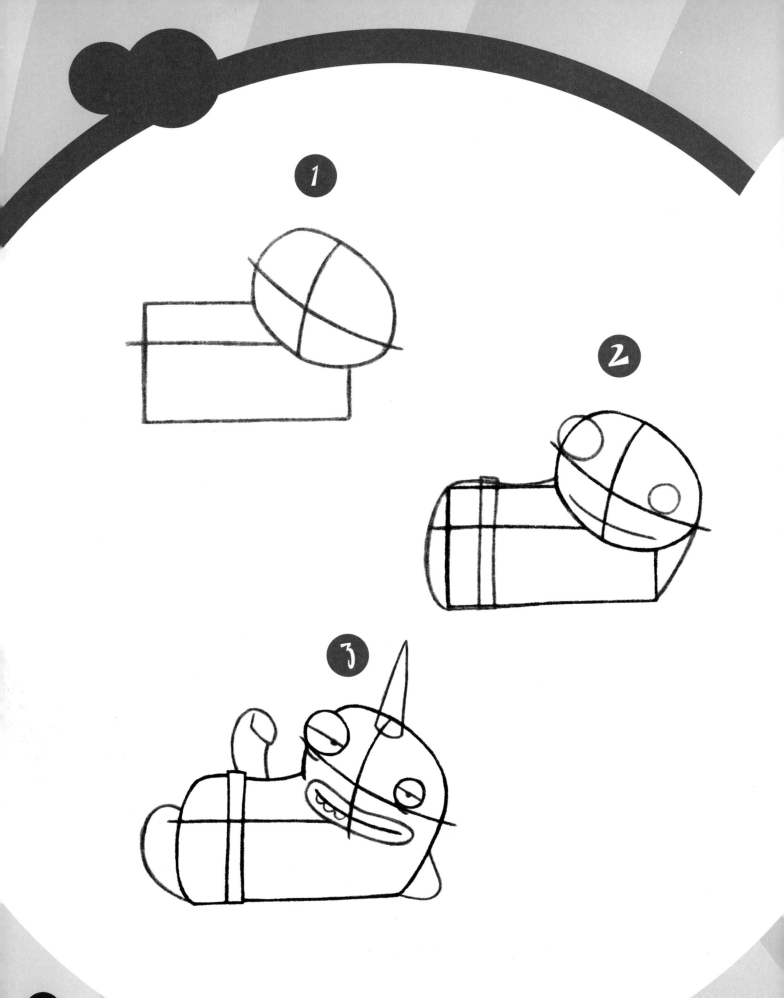

TRY MORE OF NARWHAL'S LOOKS!

"KEEP IT BUTTERY, BABY!"

PIGGY

Piggy is the intense chef at the Banana Cabana. His specialty is scooping things. Piggy takes his work very seriously and often loses his temper, making him a little scary to his coworkers. But this culinary master is a pig of great mystery, speaking with a thick accent of unknown origin.

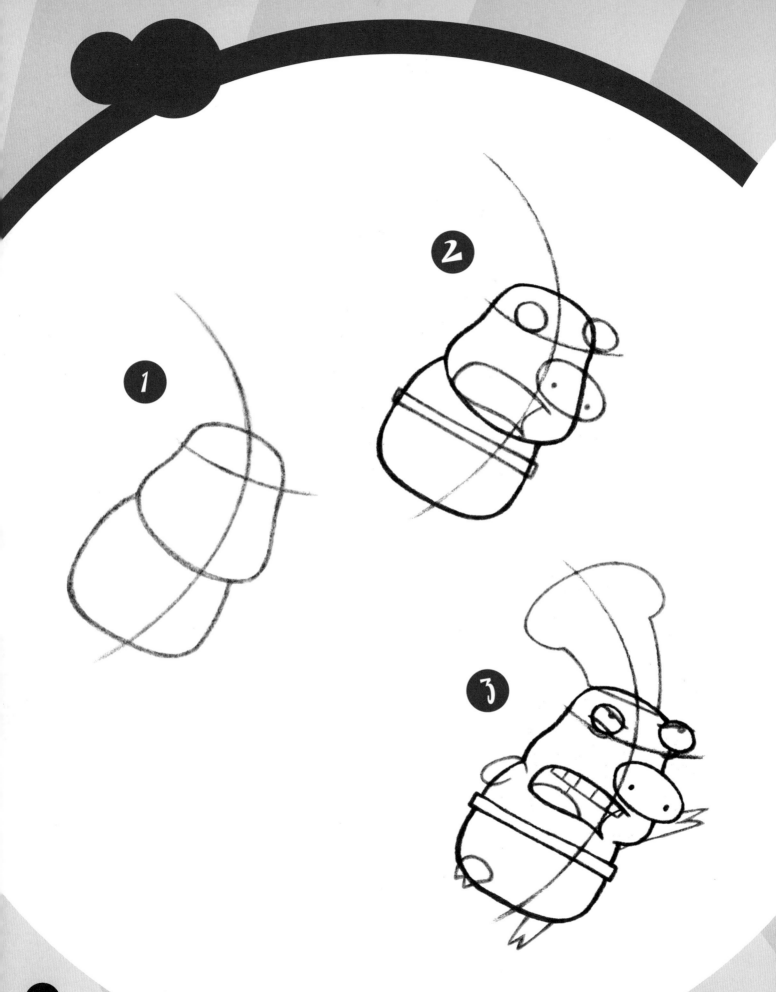

TRY MORE OF PIGGY'S LOOKS!

"I SCOOP YOU!"

SLOTH

Despite Sloth's lack of speed, she is loyal and committed—especially when it comes to Howie. No matter what insane thing he does next, Sloth will not-so-quickly "rush" to his side to tell him how amazing he is. Her other favorite things to do include getting a makeover and lounging.

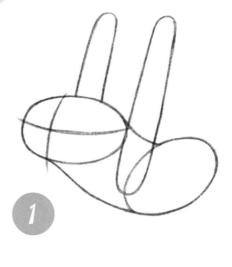

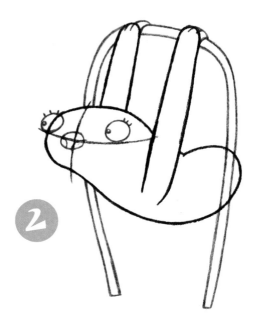

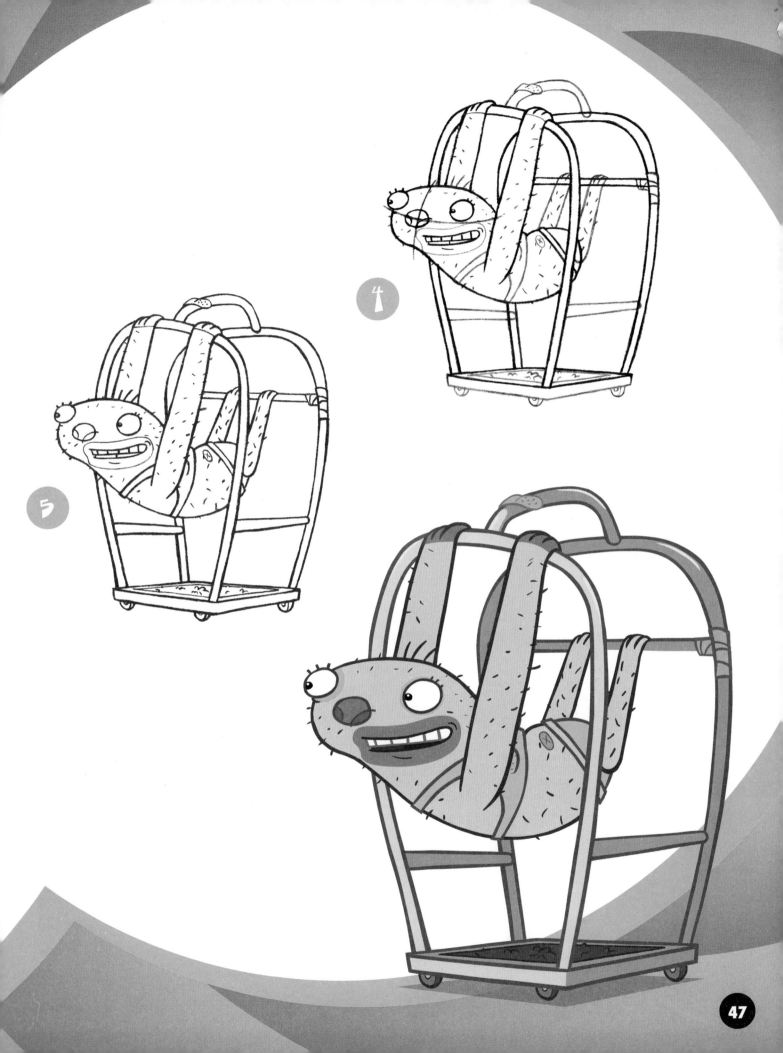

TRY MORE OF SLOTH'S LOOKS!

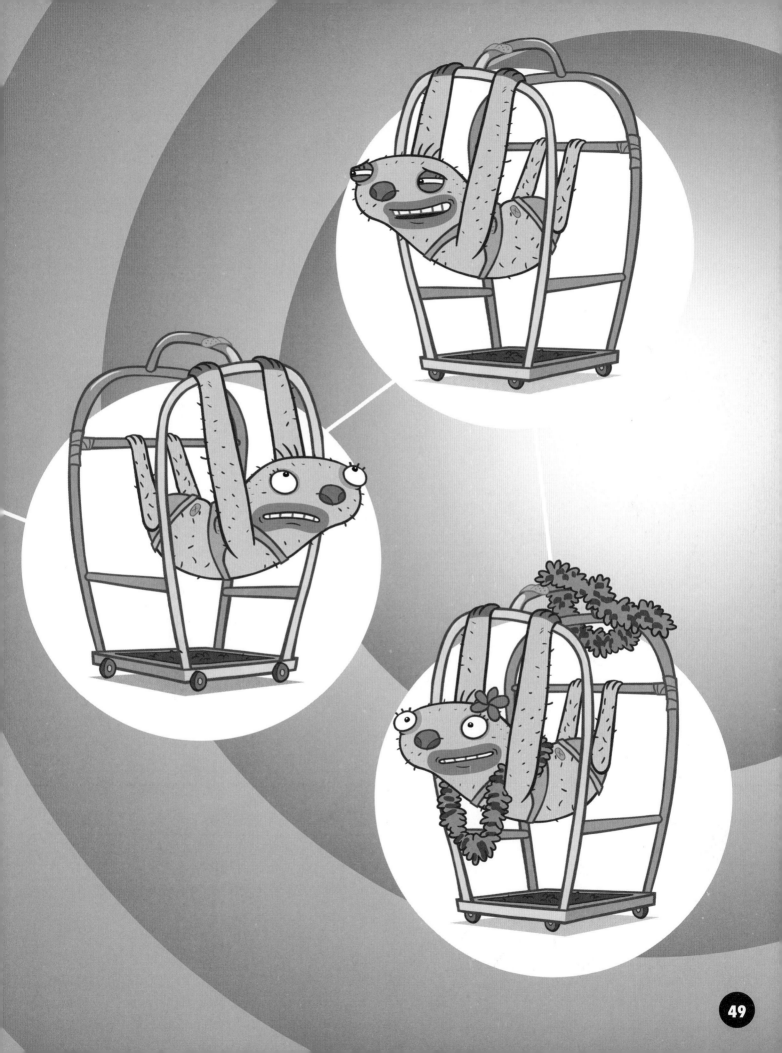

POODLE

Poodle is Howie's ruthless, scheming sister. Also in the hotel business, she runs a ritzy upper-class resort called the "Chateau Chattoo." Poodle rules with an iron-manicured paw and only cares about herself. She prefers the finer things in life— specifically custard, fountains, golden bricks, and acting like a princess.

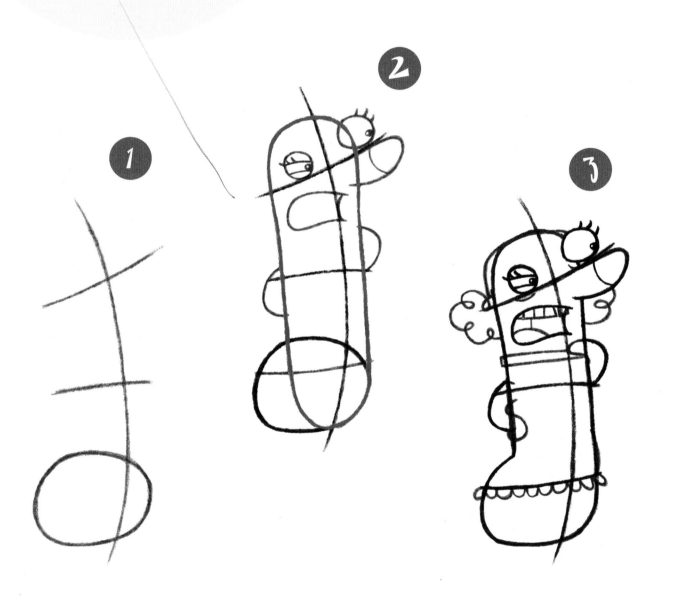

TRY MORE OF POODLE'S LOOKS!

BATTY

Batty is Poodle's devoted hench-animal. Batty speaks in a snarly-sounding voice, is extremely jumpy, not very clever, and flies about as well as a chicken. But when Poodle needs a trap-setter—whether a chauffeur, a pilot, or a manicurist—he is the bat for the job.

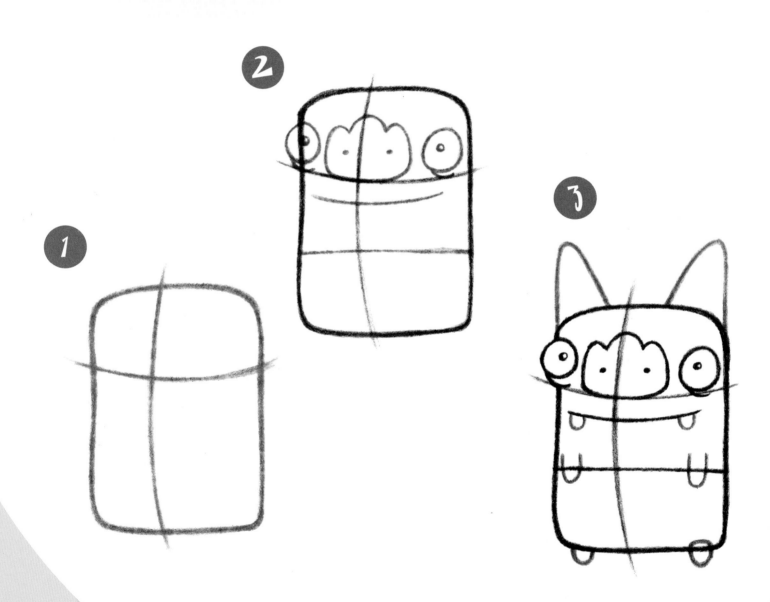

TRY MORE OF BATTY'S LOOKS!

DIRK DANGER

Dirk Danger is small in size, but giant in personality! The stunt star seems to be fearless—but that might be because he's oblivious to pain. A native of Swed-o-vlakia, Dirk is very superstitious and refuses to perform without loud polka music playing in the background.

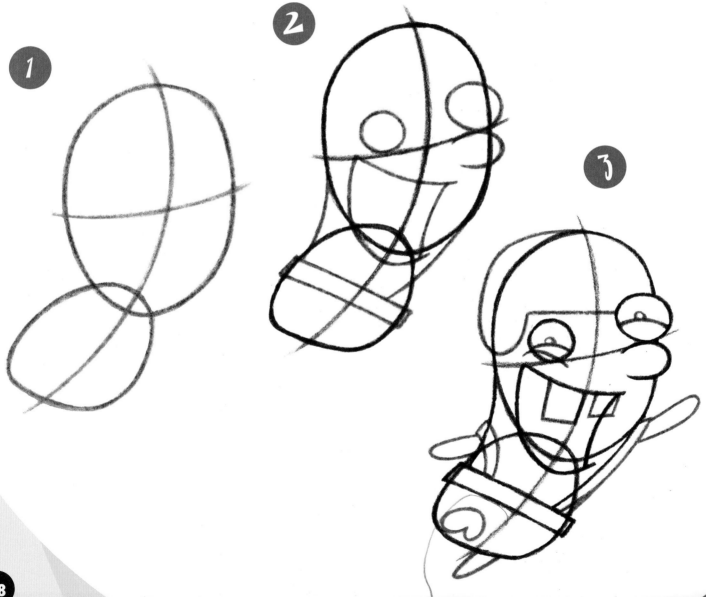

TRY MORE OF DIRK DANGER'S LOOKS!

ALMOST NAKED FRIENDS

Mammoth

Snake

Mole

Moose

Camel

Hedgehog

Crab

Bumblebee

Rooster

Squid

Cap'n Fizzy

Platypus

Shrimp

Cockroach

Yeti

Radiation Rooster

THE END

Now that you've visited the Banana Cabana and learned how to draw the Almost Naked Animals, create your own crazy adventures. Remember to use your imagination—and have fun!